A FRIENDSHIP FOR A LIFETIME

BREE BAGLEY   LAUREN HILLIARD   SHERIDAN LEE
JANIYAH THORNTON

Introduction

Bree Bagley *by Kim Bagley*

We had to rush out of the door to be on time for the first day of Pre-K4. The pleats in Bree's uniform jumper had to be pressed. Her peter pan collar had to lay perfectly over the tie she didn't want to wear. After touching up her hair and grabbing her backpack, we loaded up the car. We arrived at the school after she sat in silence buckled in the middle car seat. She always sat in the middle, between her two brothers. Where she sat in the car was not different from any other day, but where she was going would change her forever. We moved through the check-in process and landed in the place that would be her home away from home for the school year.

There were two small classrooms and a bathroom. I believe there were 16 children, whose names appeared in alphabetical order on the smart board. She spotted her name at the apple shaped table and her cute little cubby. The room was filled with chatter as everyone tried to figure out where to sit and what to do. The teacher and assistant officially welcomed the group. Parents lined up in a sort of half circle close to the wall.

I don't remember the speech, because I was gazing at my daughter and her twin brother. I didn't know who was more nervous, the kids or me. Was it too soon for "real school?" After all, Bree was still three-years old and wouldn't turn four for another month or so. She had never been in a formal classroom setting and had not spent time with a large group of children. This experience would take her from being cared for in our home and spending time exclusively with her brother to a full classroom.

I knew her brother would be fine because he was very inquisitive and outgoing. However, I was worried because Bree was quiet, always reserved, naturally cautious and had limited experiences with others. I wasn't sure how she would do in a structured learning environment. She was my sweet-faced, laid-back free spirit. But, how would she do? Would she cling to her twin brother and not make any friends? Was this the best school for her?...

As my insecurities and these questions swirled through my head, I realized it was time for the parents to leave. I didn't cry, but I wanted to. I reluctantly said my goodbyes, which included a big, long hug and a couple of "are you okays?" Bree looked up at me with her innocent eyes and nodded yes. One by one, parents left the classroom and there were tears, but none from my kids. We made our way to the exit door, and I found myself standing on the sidewalk. I couldn't make it to the car. I wasn't alone. A few other anxious parents were unable to leave so we introduced ourselves and exchanged numbers. I locked in several phone numbers in my iPhone.

I introduced myself as the mom of twins. I don't think I even told anyone their names. After we exchanged information and chatted, I felt like I could walk away with some level of comfort. It seemed other parents were also suffering from separation anxiety, so I was not alone. These parents thought all would go well since I had two children in the class. So, I focused on that as I made my way to the car and drove off the parking lot.

I was so excited when the school day came to an end, so I could ask Bree tons of questions about her day. I wanted to know each and every detail. Instead I received a few lack-luster sentences about lunch. After day one, I was very worried that this was not going to work. Who was I kidding? Bree was super sweet, but her sweetness could be easily overshadowed by her shyness. So, at the end of each day, I would check to make sure she was ok. Slowly but surely, I began to see a change. Not only was Bree learning and becoming interested in school, she slowly but surely began to open up.

I was delighted with the feedback I received from her teacher. I also loved picking Bree up from aftercare. Parents were allowed to pick up their children from the classroom and this gave me a chance to observe her interacting with others. Bree was smiling and laughing and fully engaged.

That surely wasn't the same quiet little girl who refused to talk!

My heart would skip a beat as I regularly peeked in on the class. I no longer worried if I made the right decision to put Bree in school. She was exactly where she needed to be. She was blessed to connect with several wonderful children and established and maintained an amazing relationship with three special girls: Janiyah, Lauren and Sheridan.

Today I am thrilled to see what will happen next. Who is Bree becoming and how will her story unfold? As she moves through the early stages of life, I know her foundation is solid, and there are so many interesting and amazing layers yet to be discovered. Bree is quiet and confident. She is humble and beautiful. She is kind and strong. She is cautious and adventurous. She is discerning and carefree. She is adaptable and resolute. She is joyful and serious. She is our wonderful gift from God and I am proud to call Bree my daughter.

Lauren Hilliard *by Walayna Hilliard*

Our first meeting was back-to-school orientation for the parents and children. The K-4 experience was not just exciting for the kids, but it also allowed the parents to bond and create connections as our children matriculated through their early years of school. The field trips, birthday parties and play dates created memories that will last for years to come. The commonality of faith, family and friends made the journey an enjoyable experience. Although each of the girls are no longer attending the same school, their friendships have remained consistent.

What started out as the parents' search for education has allowed these girls the opportunity to develop a relationship that represents a Christ-centered life with like-minded friends. When my husband and I made the decision to move Lauren to another school, it was not an easy decision. All she could think about was, "What about my friends? No, Mommy, I don't want to go to another school. I'm going to miss my friends." The reward of true friendship is being able to stay connected through life transitions. The early childhood development and friendships of Bree, Janiyah, Sheridan, and other K-4 friends have been purposeful. They helped to shape, develop and enhance the character of Lauren.

Lauren has several interests, such as basketball, reading, and playing the saxophone, but her passion for friends and fellowship is always a priority. She is an intelligent young lady who is passionate about learning. Some of her strongest attributes are being committed, patient, and kind. One of Lauren's qualities is that she is not judgmental and is always willing to embrace others who may be different. We are thankful to God for Lauren Nicole Hilliard. She is our gift from the Lord, and we are especially proud of her.

Sheridan Lee *by Karen Lee*

I am Sheridan Lee's Mom, and I wouldn't have it any other way. Being Sheridan's Mom means I get to know things about her that no one else does. In fact, I would like to share a few of those things with you now. First, when Sheridan was young, many people would have said that she was very shy and quiet. While it is true that she took a while to warm up when meeting new people, ultimately "quiet" has never really been a word that would most accurately describe her.

Sheridan started talking at nine-months old. Now that she is 13 years old, her ability to communicate is one of her strongest traits. She is chatty. She has a healthy intrigue with social media. She likes to engage people to ponder and discuss issues of the day. People much older than her tend to enjoy sharing a conversation with her. Her thoughts and opinions are valued. She has even shown an interest in studying broadcast journalism. I believe Sheridan's dynamic personality can actually lead her down any number of different paths in life. Sheridan has always paid attention to the news. Like many young teen girls, she likes news about fashion and entertainment. Yet also, at a surprising level for her age—she holds steadfast opinions about politics and civil rights.

Sheridan was born during the final months of Barack Obama's successful campaign to become the first African American to assume the office of President of the United States. So, she has heard his voice and seen images of him and his family from the very start. Though, even as a toddler, she was clearly more interested in Michelle Obama. Since then, several stories of racial and social injustices have been brought to the forefront within our country. I witnessed Sheridan getting riled up while watching the news when someone is unjustly ridiculed, brutalized, or treated unfairly. She has a strong sense of what we consider to be right-vs-wrong, and she is confident enough to be outspoken about that.

Her confidence has developed over time and was bolstered by the support of teachers and administrators at her school. Our family chose to enroll Sheridan in a Christian school, starting from K-4, and she has attended that same school ever since. The school educates children through the eighth grade, and we are now considering where she will attend high school. Sheridan is excited and looking forward to making new friends and realizing those high school experiences she has so often dreamed of. There is no question that the foundation laid during her early education years will continue to influence her choices. The relationships Sheridan developed there, including those with her co-authors of this book: Bree, Janiyah, and Lauren will help to shape the adult person she will eventually become.

Sheridan is bright, sensitive, and caring. She likes music, dancing, and celebrating with family and friends. To her, life should be full of fun, parties, and relaxation. Having Sheridan has made me feel happy and has given me a real sense of satisfaction as a Mom. She is a joy to know, and I truly admire her. I hope the stories and perspectives she shares in this narrative will allow numerous others to know and admire her too.

Janiyah Thornton *by LaTashia Thornton*

Where has the time gone? One moment you are being brought your newest family addition who is totally reliant on you for everything and the next instance you turn around and have a teenager. Well, it's not literally a moment, but boy that is surely how it feels! There are so many moments that you remember as a parent, and so many firsts that happen in your child's life. Not only the day they are born, there is also the first time you bring them home; their first step; first fall; first birthday; first Christmas; first day of school, and the list goes on and on.

It amazes me how our Creator so intricately put our minds together. He created it to be able to store and recall all these memories and bring them to the present, as if they happened yesterday. One memory I would like to share is the one that brought these four girls together. It was the fall of 2011, and their first orientation as they prepared to enter K-4 together. In my mind Janiyah was still too young to be left all day at school, and I wanted to hold on to the time that I had with my little girl. Those precious moments I had being her teacher at home. A part of me knew it was time, but the other part of me wanted to continue being there full-time. The time had come, however, for my husband and I to let go a little more, yet again.

There we were standing in Janiyah's classroom. Being introduced to so many new families and watching our little girl venture off to find her name plate on one of the tables, as her teacher instructed. As she found and took her seat it felt as if I was watching a movie. This movie scene was unlike any other. Although I was present in the scene my part was not a leading role. I found myself in a supporting role while in the classroom.

I looked to my right and saw my husband was observing everything as well. When I looked to my left, I witnessed the other parents watching their children with the same expression my face was showing. Our *babies* were transitioning to another phase of their lives. As a parent, this was an extremely emotional moment. One I am sure many of you can relate to. I was filled with excitement, hesitation, and a little sadness, because it's in these moments that you recognize having to let go. A little more, yet again... Once I regained my focus, I turned my eyes back to Janiyah. She was full of excitement, embracing this new phase of her life with such ease and open arms. She was fully engaged and showed no signs of concern.

It was then that I was reminded of Janiyah's greatness and the purpose placed in her by Our Father, Elohim. You see, from the time my husband and I found out we were expecting, we sought Our Father, Elohim, regarding our child's purpose and the name He wanted us to give her. Janiyah Manae means, "Bringer of Life" and "One who loves and is loved." As Janiyah sat in her seat that day, not only was she bringing life with her to share with the other children, but she was also embracing life—and all it has to offer- and loving every minute of it.

My focus immediately changed to experiencing the same joy and excitement I saw in her eyes. The Father quickly reminded me that He had her. Why would we begin doubting Him now? From the time of her birth we lifted her up and committed her life to Him. We embraced knowing that Janiyah was surely not our own. We knew and continue to know He has entrusted us with raising Janiyah to fulfill His purpose for her life, and this was all a part of the plan.

We knew we were guided to this school for a purpose. Janiyah was an eagle and now she was surrounded by other eagles who were all ready to take flight out of their nests. This was very evident to me as I took another look around the room and my perspective changed. There were some amazing children, amazing parents and amazing teachers in the room that day. This was the beginning of many friend-ships for both the children and the parents. From these friendships an extended family was formed, and many of those relationships are still intact. I am so grateful for the connections that developed over the four years Janiyah attended that school, and the genuine friendships that were able to be formed there.

These friendships have blossomed and grown over the years into the relationships you will read about on the pages of this book.

The friendships Janiyah, Lauren, Bree and Sheridan have maintained are pure and true. The commitment you all have made to sharing your story with others is something to be celebrated. You all have shown tremendous determination and commitment, both individually and collectively. My prayer is that their story will encourage many young girls to talk more freely about their feelings, experiences, and the friendships they have experienced throughout the lives. To be more accepting of others and their differences and, most importantly, to be true to their unique selves along the way.

The genuineness of their friendship and the willingness to share their experiences to encourage other young girls is so powerful. It is such a blessing to see your child has the experience of true friends, especially with so much going on in the world around us.

To our dear Janiyah, WE are so proud of you! We are proud of the young lady you have become and who you are becoming. We see the love you have for others. Your willingness to share your gifts, and the life you carry with you, will continue to reach so many. Whether you are sharing your gifts of the arts through dance, theater, music composition, crocheting or just being willing to help when needed, you soar. Keep soaring and continue to walk in truth. Your purpose will be fulfilled as you keep walking in the footsteps Elohim has ordered for you. In following the will of the Father, many more opportunities will come to you. Those doors that the Father opens will be in the perfect season and time, and you will walk through them with confidence and be successful.

Keep soaring Janiyah Manae! We will always have your back! We will always be cheering you on! We will always love you!

The Meetup

BREE

I met so many people on our first day of school, which was Pre-K4. I was actually three and I later found out that I was one of the youngest ones there because I had a late birthday. My birthday is in September and we started school in August. I really don't remember when my parents told me that we would be starting school. I just remember showing up at the school one day. I didn't really want to go because I was happy being at home with the babysitter. But everybody has to start school at some point, so it was my turn.

The first day of school I remember going inside and not saying anything. I really did not talk much my whole first year of school. Yes, I was that shy. I didn't even want to make new friends. If the teacher talked to me of course I would talk back, and if a classmate talked to me, I would do the same.

The conversation would definitely not be long at all, but I would still say something to them.

In the classroom there was a pear, grape, and apple table. I sat at the apple table with four other classmates. I liked my table mates because they were all very nice to me. We shared crayons, pencils and a little conversation. I was just getting used to everything when there was a little bit of a change. One day while taking our nap there was a flood in our classroom. We had to go to another classroom and had a new seating arrangement. So then I needed to get adjusted to a whole new group of kids. But I made it.

I liked the reading circles. That was when our teacher would sit all of us in a circle on the floor and read to us. We learned words and heard cool stories. I also liked lunch, but sometimes the class would get in trouble and then we would all get punished with silent lunch. Silent lunch was fine with me because I was quiet anyway. I wasn't all the way silent, but I was not a talkative person either.

All I know is that I would talk more at home than at school. I just was more comfortable talking with my family than at school. I didn't like the attention, and I didn't like speaking up because I did not want the entire class looking at me. I didn't even like blowing my nose in class because everyone would turn around and look. I felt like a person who turned red from being embarrassed, but you couldn't see the red on my face or cheeks. I was red on the inside.

My twin brother was the exact opposite. He was an attention-seeker. He would walk up to anyone and start talking to them, and he asked a lot of questions too. That just wasn't me. Most of my classmates were nice and easy to play with, and the teachers were nice.

I knew we were going to be at this school for a while because my family really liked the school, and we weren't really looking for anywhere else to go. I also knew I needed to talk and learn more about my classmates. So, as an entire year went by, I opened up to some and was friendly to some, but I wouldn't say I had friends. My goal was to get comfortable with everyone and it took me a while to do that. I never felt isolated or alone. I just didn't get totally comfortable.

I made a decision I needed to start figuring out what this friendship thing was all about. I will never forget the class bully. I knew I didn't want to be around anyone who behaved like her. She didn't really mess with me, but she once dragged my brother to the gym, pushed someone down the slide, and did some other really mean things to the other students.

LAUREN

When Janiyah, Bree, Sheridan and I first met, we were all facing a common obstacle: the first day of school...ever. We were all attending Pre-K at Excellence Christian School (ECS) in Maryland. Like most kids in our grade, we were at least four or five. At the time we were the *only* Pre-K class, so we were kind of trailblazers for our future graduating class of 2025. We were one single pack... of gum, wolves or whatever you want to call it.

The classroom was conjoined. Two rooms connected by a bathroom with two doors on the sides. We were living a luxury in that classroom. There was a closet that somehow held enough cots for nap time, and three fruit-shaped tables: apple, grape, and pear. As you know, we were a bunch of random kids who were fully reliant on our parents. That were now being handed off to a really tall woman with a bunch of other kids, who have no clue what's going on.

You may be thinking, "You are total strangers, how did you get along and birth such an amazing friendship?" Well... that's the point of this book, but anyway, some of the significant events that were helpful to this breath-taking friendship were *the adventures of pre-k*. There was the discovery and introduction to an odd substance called *oobleck*. Oobleck is a mixture of cornstarch and water with properties of both a solid and a liquid.

Of course, four-year old me had no idea what any of those items were. So, to see that it had the same properties of the juice I drank that morning, and the bed frame that I had fallen off of a couple days ago, blew all sixteen of our little pea brains into bits.

Along with the discovery of oobleck, we also participated in *show-and-tell*. I don't really remember what everyone else had, but I brought a harmonica that I got from my granddad. I didn't know how to play it, but I had seen in the movies where they blew into one and it made a noise. Of course, in the movies it was musical and pleasing to the ears. So, I tried to recreate the musical essence of the harmonica. I did it no justice, but I was proud, nonetheless. Afterwards, we played in the classroom for the rest of the afternoon, and I became the female embodiment of Bob the Builder. Ahh, fun times.

SHERIDAN

Hi, my name is Sheridan Lee, and I am in eighth grade. This book is written by my friends and me. This story is about each of our different experiences through school. I'll start you off with a little bit of background. We started out as friends when we were four, and we all went to the same school. Over time our parents and extended family got the chance to know each other as well. Once we reached the second grade, we remained friends and have continued being friends over the years, despite ending up in different schools.

We decided to meet up every month just to talk and have fun. One month, we decided to start writing this book based on our experiences with leaving the school. Or, in my case, staying at the school.

As the others may have mentioned, we met on the first day of school in our K-4 homeroom. I can't remember exactly when we met, but I imagine it being during recess. Recess was always fun. We had a specific mulch on the playground which consisted of wood, and it had a bunch of dust. Whenever it was windy outside, the dust would get in our eyes and we would struggle to find our friends. It sounds tragic but it really just added to the excitement of playing outside. Kids would run all over the place while the teachers told us how much time we had left at recess before we had to go to our next class.

What may have allowed us and our parents to really connect were the field trips. Our class often visited the Smithsonian Museum in D.C, because that was closest to where we lived. That was where most of our field trips were. We were all on the bus together, socializing and exploring the city of D.C. I felt our field trips were a great time for the class to get along and learn outside of the school. We also didn't have to do class work.

K-4 was our first year at Excellence. For some of us it was our first year in school. I attended a daycare center before I came to ECS. My daycare experience was interesting. My parents tell me this story all the time.

On the first day I was nervous because I didn't want to leave my parents. Once we got to the daycare center, I had a good time. I played on the playground and even made a friend. Keep in mind that before I was going to daycare, I would go to my grandparent's house every day. We passed their house on the way to my daycare each morning.

On my second day, I was convinced daycare was just a one-time thing, and I would be back at my grandparent's house the next day. I was wrong. We would pass my grandparent's house every day and I would scream, "No! Their house is there, Mom. Don't pass it. *It's right there*! Mom, look... *look*. No, it's coming up. *No, you passed it.*" Then I would cry the rest of the way to daycare. I did this every day for a month.

I left my daycare center on my birthday that year (my birthday is in August). I could honestly say that was a wonderful gift. I got to go to a new school and meet my friends the next week. Even though I had a rough start at my daycare, I learned the basic things I needed to know before going to school.

There was something different about Excellence Christian School. Everyone was so welcoming to the students and the parents. It felt comfortable. At the young age of four, I realized this is a good place to meet good people and make good friends. I was absolutely right. I am now in my final year at ECS, and I realize this has been a great experience.

I'm sure our parents could tell you how emotional that was for them. Seeing their little ones who now seemed to be all grown up—going to K-4 by themselves. Fortunately for us, we all became friends easily. It was not just the four of us, but our whole class. From the very beginning there was a close bond there with us all.

I remember in K-4 we had assigned seats. The tables were set up like fruits. There was an apple, grape, and pear table. I sat at the pear table. This table was closest to the board so when the teacher was teaching, I had one of the best seats. I have a specific memory from nap time with our teacher. I was really missing my parents that day, so I woke up and she asked me if I was ok. I told her what was going on and she let me sit with her for the rest of nap time. Our class also had an assistant teacher. She was much younger and is still a teacher at the school.

After our parents met each other, we were then able to go to each other's houses, and birthday parties, etc. Like most things in life, the party has to stop. In our case though, the party never stopped. We just came back for an after party, you could say. Janiyah left school after the second grade. At this point, she was the first person who left. But we all continued to stay friends. We obviously just couldn't see each other every day like we used to.

JANIYAH

The time frame that us girls met was in 2011. It was the assembly prior to the first day of school, and everyone was bustling with excitement. We were all around four years old. My first encounter with Lauren was when I was exploring the classroom. I found my way over to the kitchen play set and Lauren happened to be there. We didn't talk much, just smiled and walked away. That's how I am with most people. If it's a stranger, I just smile and then look or walk away. My first encounter with Sheridan was when she was sitting at a table and, again, I smiled and walked away. My first encounter with Bree was different. She was standing alone (she was kind of shy) and I said, "Hi."

She didn't respond.

The special event that brought us together was the annual assembly. You know, the meeting where every child and their parents come to check out the school, the teachers, and the environment. I remember seeing hallways filled with strangers; the Principal walking down the halls, and teachers conversing with parents. Burgundy, white and grey was everywhere (those were the school colors), and cases filled with trophies and pictures of past students who attended the school.

I remember hearing the Principal in the auditorium speaking effortlessly; parents whispering, and the static from the security guard's walkie-talkies, making sure everyone was in caring hands. There was the scent of new furniture. It also smelled sweet because of the cakes, cookies, and punch we were going to have after the assembly. Just the sugary scent had me bouncing in my seat with excitement.

Afterward, the only thing I tasted was the delicious, moist cake, the chewy cookies and drank some punch.

I also recall touching my parent's hands, which were soft, warm and very comforting. I was fidgeting with my clothes because I felt nervous, excitement, and curiosity, but I was also experiencing feelings of fear and anxiety. I felt unprepared.

My parents and I entered the classroom. My gaze scanned the room, landing on the odd looking chairs. I walked to one of them and felt its bumpy texture. Even though I was nervous, my new teacher gave me confidence that everything would be okay.

I also remember the look my parents on their faces. I could read the questions in their expressions.

"Will she be okay?"

"Can she handle it?"

I had some of the same questions swirling around in my head. But the more I got to know everyone, the more comfortable I felt. I knew my parents would give me the courage to face my fear. During my K-4 year, I cried because of my fear and because I missed my parents. My teachers and fellow students made me feel at home. My K-4 teacher gave me many hugs that year and always told me it was going to be alright.

Connection Point

BREE

My first connections with some of the girls happened at recess and aftercare. That's when we could run and play, and just have fun. Janiyah was good friends with Ana, another girl in our class. I was a little jealous of Janiyah because she had a close friendship with Ana, and I wanted to have a friendship like theirs. I started to spend more time with some of the girls in my class, and Janiyah became one of my first friends. I soon became friends with Ana and Briana too.

Janiyah was fun and liked to joke around. We had fun playing tag, hide-and-seek, board games, puzzles and *Uno*. I was also on the track team with Janiyah. I didn't like going to practice much. Actually I made up excuses. The best thing about being on the track team was I enjoyed racing with Janiyah and my other friends.

One day, while playing hide-and-seek, I was one of the hiders and one of my new friends was the seeker. I was hiding under the chair and she was standing on the top of the chair. She said, "I found you," and then jumped down. She jumped directly on my right hand, which is my dominant hand. It didn't really hurt that bad at first, but she started crying even before I cried. I guess it was because we were close, and she was sad that she'd hurt me. She showed me what it meant to have a friend who cares.

Later, the pain started kicking in and I started crying. She was still crying when my mom came to pick me up. When we got in the car, I told her what happened, and then we went to Patient First. My arm was fractured, and I had to wear a bandage.

The next day, I went back to school. Before going into the classroom, I cried, because I had to do everything with my left hand, and I thought my arm was going to be messed up forever. But I also felt good because my classmates were so nice and tried to help me. Everyone signed my bandage. This was another way that I knew I had good friends.

In addition to going to regular classes, we had Chapel lessons. One day our kindergarten class was supposed to lead Chapel. The Chapel teacher stopped in our class and asked if there were any dancers. Sheridan and I both raised our hands. Then the teacher asked us both to join a group in the hallway. So, we immediately went from sitting in class to joining the dance team to do a dance. We were in the hallway learning choreography.

That's when I first connected with Sheridan. We were

practicing and learning our dance and we began to bond during our practices. We both had a love of dance and I think that is what helped us to bond. Plus, she is super sweet. She danced for a competitive dance company and so did I. We both spent lots of time after school at practices. I even saw Sheridan at a couple of dance competitions.

Aftercare was one of the best times in the school day. It was a mix of recess, playtime and a little schoolwork. One day, Lauren, Joe and I were in aftercare and started to make a rap. We were making up random songs to a beat and it was fun. Joe was beating on the desk and Lauren and I were laughing and rapping. That's when I first started to talk to Lauren. We did not sit together, but we had fun in aftercare. Especially, since we were one of the last kids to be picked up by our parents.

I also was on the cheer squad with Lauren. So, we would learn our cheers at our after-school practices. We would also sit together after the basketball games and eat our snacks, which was always a good treat. My friendship with Lauren grew and we had many playdates at her house. She had a swing set and lots of room to play, and she had no brothers! So, we got to have fun without being around the boys.

Lauren also spent time with me during my dance competitions. Dance competitions lasted all day long, and we might only have a few 2–3-minute dances. But Lauren was a patient and understanding friend. She had a book and some snacks and was supporting me the entire time. She played basketball, and I went to some of her basketball games. I liked being around Lauren because she was calm and had a funny side that makes me laugh.

LAUREN

When our friend group met, we were not always besties. We had our class as a whole and then there were some sub-divisions of kids that were almost duos. I don't remember my first encounter with Bree and Sheridan, but I do remember my first experience with Janiyah. Two of my classmates were "fighting" on the playground, and I remember being told to be Janiyah's buddy, since it was her first day.

To be honest, I wouldn't even call it a fight because it lasted less than two minutes. I wasn't even aware of it until we turned the corner of the playground. I didn't know what to do with that information, so I just went with it and was like, "...and this is the fight..." like it was planned or something. Although soon after, our teachers pulled them apart.

Our entire class was just like, "Awww..." and then proceeded to carry on with recess like nothing happened. Afterwards, we got called to the Principal's office. I'm pretty sure four out of 15 of us were crying because we got in trouble... I may or may not have been one of them. Quite a memory indeed!

Of course, those duos soon grew into all of the girls in the class. There were 15 kids in our class, and we were split half and half gender-wise. Eight boys and seven girls. By the third grade, I'd say that all of us were pretty well acquainted.

One thing I remember was playing "family" during recess

every day. We had a single mother, solely because all the boys were trying to be the next Lebron James. A lot of times Sheridan would be the baby, Bree and Janiyah would be like older siblings, and I would be some weird animal. I remember being a tiger once (I don't know, I was in third grade).

Another thing about third grade was that they allowed us to bring our electronics out during lunch time. So, we would walk in the cafeteria; place our devices where we sat; grab our food; eat quickly and then see who was the best at a certain game. For the longest time that game was *Rolling Sky*. It then shifted to *Jetpack Joyride*, *Temple Run* or *Talking Tom* or *Angela*. But *Rolling Sky* held supreme. We would have a little competitions to see who the best.

Another memory I remember was from aftercare, where we would do homework for 45 minutes and then we were free to roam the classroom. Some kids would spin beyblades inside the desks, and some would be playing electronic games on their devices. Meanwhile we would make paper creations and origami. After that, we would go to the gym and play tag for a good hour or until everyone left. It was our version of 'playing until the streetlights came on'. It was fun.

SHERIDAN

If I remember correctly, I was not the first to introduce myself. I could imagine it being Lauren or Janiyah. They were the most talkative, I feel. Bree was super quiet at the time. I know that our class was tight for the most part. I really enjoyed our class. As I said before, I think our class and the four of us mostly bonded over recess and field trips back then.

As we got older, we bonded over different things like birthday parties. At some point, all four of us danced; either at a studio or for the school. That was something we all bonded over, and then our parents all knew each other, so we really got to hang out more after that. We had some play dates when we were younger but mostly parties. Those would either be with the whole class or just the girls in the class.

The thing about Excellence though is that when we were younger all of these different events would happen. For example, I'm not sure if other schools did this, but we would have Dr. Seuss Day, where the lunch ladies made green eggs and ham like in the Dr. Seuss story. I remember when we were younger most of us wondered how they got the eggs to be green. Eventually one of the teachers told us that they used green food dye.

Every few months we would have a group of actors come to the school and act out skits about someone's life. That was always cool. I always learned something new. Our school field trips were fun too. But we always went to the same places: The National Aquarium, The Smithsonian National Air and Space Museum, The Smithsonian National Museum of Natural History... but when we kept going, it became boring. I think the teachers noticed, and we started to go to different places.

On class field trips, we would often break into groups. Typically, boys were in one group and girls in another. The four of us were usually in a group. It would always be funny wherever we saw another group of kids who went to our school in the museum. We would act like we hadn't seen each other in years even though we saw each other on the bus.

The souvenir shop was fun. Most times I would get something that was completely unrelated to the field trip. Sometimes I would get candy, but usually something small just to fidget with on the bus ride back to school. I, personally, would fall asleep on the way back. I liked to sit on the window seat when our class went on field trips. Especially when we were driving to the museum. I could see all the people driving to work in the morning, with their coffee and work clothes. When sitting on the bus I would look down on people, so I would feel much taller than what I actually am.

JANIYAH

This is our tenth anniversary of being friends. We have been friends ever since we were little things. The fact that we are still friends today amazes me. I love all of my friends dearly. All of us did not become instant friends. We took time to learn about each other every day.

We enjoyed the times we laughed on the bus or played games on the playground. Even when it was quiet time after lunch, we smiled across the room. They even helped me when I was afraid of a school mascot. When I cried, all of my classmates gave me a hug. They comforted me.

In first grade, Sheridan and I liked to watch a specific TV show and then talk about it when we came back to school.

But eventually she stopped watching it, and then we didn't really have anything else to talk about. I was honestly sad and cried to my mom about it after school. We now have TV streaming services, so Sheridan and I can watch and talk about our favorite shows. We also had dance practices at the same studio for about a year.

Lauren and I liked to read all the books in the classroom. We also liked to play games or do research in the almost empty computer room. We were even on the same dance team at school. And when we created and made our own games in kindergarten, Bree and I played each other's games and had a lot of fun. Another fun thing that I did with Sheridan, Bree, or Lauren was go up to the cafeteria and bring the teacher her lunch every day.

In first grade our teacher built a bat cave and we all would go to the computer room and take notes on what we learned, and then talk about it. We all were on the cheer team together. We were also on the track team for two years.

We saw each other so much and over the years we created this sort of bond between us. On field day Sheridan and I were on the same team. We got to spend the whole day together. It was something that was unique to us. When I connected with each of my friends, I felt like we would be friends forever. It was like they were my family and school was my home away from home.

Who We Are

BREE

My name is Bree Micah, and I am the only girl in my family. I have a twin brother and an older brother. I have always wanted an older sister, but I am lucky to have a twin. Even though he can be annoying and is the complete opposite of me, I know he will always be there for me. We don't look alike, so most people don't realize we are twins. In school, our classmates didn't know.

My parents met in college and have been married a long time. They decided, after having one child, that they wanted one more. And they got us! So, we are close, but all very different. My parents teach us to love and support each other and always have each other's back.

Family is very important, and I love that I always have my brothers. I feel very protected in a family of all boys and they are fun too. They can play wild and rough, but they have taught me how to be tough. I have also spent lots of time watching my brothers play baseball and basketball. In addition to cheering them on at games, I've also participated in my own activities.

My extended family is located in Baltimore and Virginia. We don't get to see each other as much as I would like, and usually spend time together at our big Thanksgiving gatherings. That's when a big group of us (more boy cousins) get together and have the very best meal ever. My uncle Tony makes a special treat just for me, chitterlings and I love it. My grandmother and I are the only ones who eat them. My uncle Jerome makes the best chocolate chip cookies, and I can't count how many cookies I eat on Thanksgiving Day.

Easter is also big in my family, and we always have an Easter egg hunt. Every year, I usually find the most eggs. My grandparents, known as Pop Pop and Grams, send gifts and cards and treats in the mail. They make us feel special, even when they are not able to visit.

I wish I had known my maternal grandmother, who passed away when my mother was pregnant with us. I used to dream about her. My mother says she loves me, even from Heaven, and I am very special because I am her only granddaughter.

The best way to describe me is athletic, calm, and a loyal friend. I am very observant and like to check things and people out before I talk to them. But once someone gets to know me, they see just how cool I am. I have participated in many activities. At first, my dad tried to get me to play basketball, but I didn't want to do it. One of my brother's coaches wanted to train me because he said I had natural ability. But I just didn't want to play. I was a cheerleader for my school, and I liked that, but I really loved dancing.

I started dancing when I was five years old. I moved from recreational dancing to competitive dance. It gave me the chance to travel to Las Vegas, Orlando, Myrtle Beach, Ocean City and lots of other places. I am proud that the wall in my room has several trophies and medals that I won from dancing with my group, and in solos.

My first solo dance was a tap dance to Frank Sinatra's *New York, New York*. That's because New York is one of my favorite places. I love New York, but I actually forgot the dance before I went on stage. My teacher saved me because she was backstage doing all the moves, so I made it through.

I always had butterflies, fears and would overthink my routine before I went on stage, but all of those feelings would go away as soon as I started dancing. It has been my absolute favorite thing to do, and jazz is my favorite type of dance. It makes me feel free and lets me express my emotions and feelings. I also loved changing into pretty costumes and wearing makeup.

I ran track for a couple of years and liked it, but I always wanted to learn another sport. I'm interested in playing volleyball and started learning more about it in clinics. I think it would be a good sport for me since I'm tall and I can jump. Plus, I want to stay active. So it's something that I want to get better at and play in high school. But I always will love to dance.

I spent several years as a Girl Scout. I learned sisterhood and how to serve the community. We made arts and crafts, did slime science projects, created vision boards, visited senior citizens, and did lots of community service projects. We also learned how to have a business by selling lots of cookies. My mother was a leader and she made sure I had the chance to do all the different activities. Even though my schedule was always busy with other activities.

My favorite activity was when all of the girls spent the night outdoors in a huge tent. We watched movies, played games and stayed up as long as we could. We even got rained on, but it didn't stop me from having fun. I'm not a big movie watcher, but I love watching TV cooking shows. My television stays on the cooking network all day and night.

I like to try some of the cooking and baking recipes. My favorite thing to do is bake cookies and brownies. I start by learning a recipe and then I can make them my own way. My cookies don't last long because my family usually eats them up in one day.

My favorite subjects in school are social studies and science. I like learning about science, and I hope to become a veterinarian since there are not many African American in this field of medicine. I know it will be hard, but I can do it. I have always loved caring for animals. We have even looked at colleges that have good animal science programs, so I can plan my future.

LAUREN

Hi! My name is Lauren. You don't really know me, but that's the whole point of this chapter. I'm a 13-year-old girl in the eighth grade. I'm an only child, and I live with both of my parents. My mom's side is much larger than my dad's side of the family, so I usually spend holidays in at least 3 different houses: my own house; my grandma's house, and my granny's house (there IS a difference). Of course, that does not mean three times more food or gifts. Since I don't have any siblings, my cousins fill these roles. Although we don't live under the same roof and we're not together all the time, when family gatherings come it's always a great time.

One of the things I enjoy doing is reading. There was a summer where I read at least seven books (willingly). I also love building *Lego* creations. I used to make little houses (that were architecturally incorrect) and come up with stories and plot lines between the *Lego* characters. I would include my different builds into the plot, which would often result in them being broken by yours truly. As of now I just make stuff and keep them intact.

I also play basketball. I've been playing basketball since I was eight, so about six years now. I was introduced to basketball in third grade, so whenever I wasn't on all fours, pretending to be a pet, I was also trying to become the next Lebron James—the *female* embodiment, of course. In fourth grade, they created a girls' basketball team and it was pretty small. There were times when we would play against boys during our regular season. I soon went to an Upward league, which was a small Christian sports league that allowed kids to play and learn true sportsmanship. Our team was undefeated.

To be honest, that was probably the best introduction to the game for me, since I had so much fun playing. For the next couple of years, I would play on a hardcore travel team. Where the "team" part of basketball was nice, the actual game was kind of lackluster. Our team was pretty good, but since I didn't get much playing time, it was just *eh*.

The worst part about it was I really tried to "get better," but the coaches never noticed. Whenever I would be in the game, I would become a nervous wreck and "mess up the flow of the team." There was one game where I accidentally scored on the wrong basket and got benched for the rest of the game. Luckily, I got cut from the team, and you may be thinking, "Lauren that's not a good thing. You should be sad." It's not that I wasn't, but I think I was more relieved that it was finally over.

As for school, I used to go to the same school as Janiyah, Sheridan, and Bree. There I think I established my first non-biological family. In fifth grade, I transitioned to another school–not too far from my old one–where I played the violin for a year and then I was introduced to the saxophone. My earlier friendships at Excellence have helped me to navigate and meet new friends at my new schools.

SHERIDAN

I am currently 13 years-old and in the eighth grade. I live with my mom and my dad and I have a sister who is 12 years older—she and I are very close. My favorite memory with her is when we went to Disney World for my fifth birthday. My family and I were walking around the park, and there was a dance party going on. The song *Call Me Maybe* by Carly Rae Jepson was hot and popular in 2012. My sister and I danced in the middle of the park while my dad recorded us. We danced until the song was over and it was dark outside.

I spent most of my childhood growing up with my extended family. I am very close with them too. We do a lot together. I am close in age with my cousin. We are only a year apart from one another. I have always been close with my grandparents. They are some of the sweetest people I know. My aunt is always there when I need a phone call. My family and I meet up for pretty much every holiday: Easter, Thanksgiving, Christmas, everything!

My sister is 25, so she has her own place now and a job. I'm so proud of her. We have many more memories together, but that one is my favorite. My saddest memory with my sister was when she went to college. I actually didn't go with her the first time, but visited after she had there for about a month.

Her school was having a family weekend, so our family went to visit her. In my five to six-year-old mind, I thought we were there to take her back home. She had been there so long that I missed her. We had a great time at family weekend but, when it was time to go, I realized she had to stay. My parents and I went back home, and I cried in the car for about an hour. My sister called to check on me because she knew I was sad about leaving her, so the whole family shed at least one tear, just hearing my sobs from the back seat.

When I was younger, I was an active dancer at a studio. I danced from ages three to nine, and eventually stopped because I wanted to try new things. I definitely missed dance and it took some getting used to when I wasn't going. In the seventh grade, I became co-captain of the cheer team, and a member of the National Junior Honor Society.

Now that I'm in the eighth grade, it is harder to participate because of COVID-19. But I'm still trying to make the most of my time. Of our group, I was the one to stay at the school. After most of my friends left, it was hard for me. I missed them. Over time, I realized that maybe they left for a reason and their families thought this was the best option. In order to be a good friend, you have to always support them and still be able to communicate. Even though it was hard for me and I missed them, we still got to see each other.

When I stayed at ECS, I was able to establish myself in the class. I felt like I stood out a little bit more than I did before.

JANIYAH

Sup! My name is Janiyah Manae Thornton. I'm 13 now, turning 14 in June and going to the ninth grade in September. I am the oldest child in my family, and I have two younger siblings. One brother and one sister. I don't want my family dynamic to ever change. I think my parents are pretty cool. They support me in everything I want to accomplish and complete.

I love my grandparents and my great-grandfather. I don't know what I'd do without them. I enjoy talking to them. We talk about when they were younger, laugh about anything, and I hang out with them whenever they visit me or when I visit them.

Boy, do I have a lot of hobbies and interests! I like to perform which includes acting, singing, and dancing. I have been singing and dancing forever, but I have been taught ballet, tap, hip-hop, jazz, lyrical, contemporary and other styles of dance for eleven years. I have also been acting ever since I was five.

I like to crochet, too. Before you even think about it… Bruh… Crochet is not something that only Grandmas like to do. Okay? It is a way to express creativity, dexterity, and hand-eye coordination skills.

I also like to jam and play guitar, a little bass, ukulele, and piano. I have played piano ever since I was five. I might not be classically trained, completely, but I did teach myself the basics. Like chords, notes, riffs, and scales, I am also self-taught on the guitar, ukulele, and bass. I hope to expand into the drums someday. I also write my own pieces.

I enjoy being outside. Bike riding, roller skating, skateboarding, scootering, and even taking nice jogs on the trail that is in my neighborhood. When I play outside and I am riding my bike, or another one of my vehicles of transportation, I look at the trees and the sun. Looking at nature gives me a sense of peace.

My favorite color is purple. All hues and shades of it. I think purple is very aesthetic. I transferred from my private school in third grade and have been homeschooled for six years. It will be seven years in September. It is hard to believe I have been doing it for that long. I love to learn, and I aspire to learn more, I have enjoyed every year of my schooling, and I am very excited for the upcoming school years.

This year has been the best, as far as our schedules go. It took us a while to get where we are, but we got there. It was hard for me to leave my friends, teachers, extracurricular activities and the feeling of going to school. My favorite subject is Math because I like to solve problems. Math is the only subject where you do not just learn the facts, but are able to do them on your own. That is what excites me about this subject.

The year of 2020 has been a rollercoaster I'll never forget. I didn't get to see my friends almost every week like I used to. I spent more time with my family, mainly my siblings, more than anyone else. Many times, I was asked to play in the basement, or outside, with their toys, and much more. But it has been a lot of fun. I am definitely a kid-at-heart and I want to be this way forever.

I enjoy doing things that 13-year-olds today may think are childish. I disagree because I have fun. I am glad to have friends like Bree, Lauren, and Sheridan, who are just like me. We enjoy the times we spend together.

I have learned that I like to have a little alone time, for myself. Whether it is playing my piano in my room or drinking a cup of tea and sitting on the couch, or watching one of my favorite TV shows. This is a special time just for me. Don't get me wrong, I do like to play with my siblings, but I cannot be around them all the time. Giving myself that time is its own reward.

All Friends Fight

BREE

Friendships come and go. I had a close friend from our old school. We were very close, and she invited me to all of her parties. We would talk on the phone 24/7 and played video games together all the time. Around sixth grade our friendship began to change. I felt like she was acting differently. She was not the ideal person I wanted to be friends with and did not act the way she used to.

She said I should be her only friend and got upset whenever I talked to other people, especially when she wanted to talk. This happened even if I talked to her for *hours*. She just didn't want me to spend time with my other friends. I still went on and talked to my other friends because I wasn't going to let anyone control me.

We went back and forth and she constantly did the same

thing and I kept letting it slide. It got extremely annoying, so I told her I didn't want to be friends anymore. She got mad when I told her that. I ended up blocking her from calling me. When I finally unblocked her, it showed she'd been texting me every day, saying, "Hey... hey Bree," or "Hey, I know you're still mad, but I will keep texting you." I was over the friendship so I didn't respond.

Almost a year later, without talking, a friend from our old school invited us to a party. A few weeks before the party I received a text from her and she said, "Act like we are still friends when you go to the party." I didn't respond.

I arrived at the party before her. When she got there, one of my friends already knew that Allison and I were no longer friends. Our mutual friend tried to get us to be friends again because we had been close friends since we were little kids. I just said, "Ok." She asked if we could play a video game online that night when we got home. I responded, "Sure," but our friendship wasn't the same anymore. After playing a game for about 30 minutes, I hung up. We haven't spoken since that day. I know that some friends grow apart and there's no one to blame. It just happens.

Another one of my friendships changed because we didn't have the same interests anymore. In the beginning of my friendship with Sierra, we liked to play *Roblox* in fifth grade. *Roblox* was not trending or exciting anymore and we got bored. We would call each other and not play *Roblox*, but our conversations was either boring or we just sat in silence. In my head I would think, "Wow, was *Roblox* the only thing that gave us something to talk about?" We ended up not talking at all, or calling each other because it was boring.

I don't have many fights with friends. I know that some friendships don't last. I try to stay out of my friends' problems. So, if my friends are having any issues, I don't get in the middle. I stay away from fights and disagreements.

All friends have little disagreements over things. My way of working through disagreements is by not getting emotional and arguing. Most of the time, my friends can easily move on from whatever is bothering them. Forgiving someone is not really hard for me, however it becomes a struggle if the individual did something really cruel to me. In this instance, I would forgive but stop talking to them. I would just drift away without making it a big deal.

The only fights I have had were with my twin brother. We fight every single day. He always has to say something smart. Then we end up yelling and arguing with each other. He will come into my room just to bother me and can never mind his own business. He does things like turn my fan off and leave with the door wide open. He makes me mad every day. He can never go a day without trying to fight or argue with me. So, yes, everyone fights.

LAUREN

Honestly, our group never really fought, but I have had disagreements with my other friends, and witnessed others debate between themselves. For example, (as mentioned in Chapter 2) with the two classmates who were fighting... we didn't really know how to respond to it. Most of us had never seen one up close. Then a classmate started chanting, *"fight, fight fight."* I guess that was when it clicked for me. "Oh! So, this is like what we see in the movies! *Fight, fight, fight."*

No one actually said what I was thinking, but that was my thought process at least. So, as said in Chapter 2, we just went with it. (Heh heh, it's fun to quote yourself.) As for how it affected me, I really don't think it did too much. I'm an only child, so seeing people fighting was foreign to me. My cousins never did any physical fighting—just name calling (I somehow earned the nickname of Ni-hao Kai-lan, which arguably was a good show, but that's a conversation for later).

Anyway, after that tussling between the two toddlers, we were sent to the Principal's office and told that we shouldn't have encouraged them by chanting. At the time, I think the only information I retained from the conversation was to not yell, "fight, fight, fight…" if you see someone fighting. As of now, I know better to try and stop it rather than encouraging it.

I remember another disagreement I had with a friend from church. It wasn't a full-out arguing match. We were really passive-aggressive with each other and it took only 30 minutes for us to apologize to each other. I think in conclusion-excluding those instances and minuscule arguments I've experienced over small topics; we never really fought with each other.

SHERIDAN

Friends have disagreements. That is normal in a healthy friendship. Even when our group was younger, we would have disagreements. Other kids in our class fought sometimes, mostly the boys. What is most important is that if you really are friends, then you should be able to forgive each other and make up. This is not always the case though.

One thing I have learned from other experiences is that it is possible for people to outgrow each other. Being the age we are now, 13 or 14-year-olds, kids try to fit in with everyone else or who they think is *cool*. They might ditch the friends that have always been with them. The phrase: *"Be Yourself"* was one of the hardest lessons I personally had to learn.

The reason why I think this was so hard for me to learn was that I hadn't really figured out my personality yet. How could you be yourself when you don't know half of your personality? Teen years are the time to find yourself and make mistakes and memories that you can eventually tell your kids someday. At least, that's what I hear. I struggled with this phrase because I developed insecurities, which happens to a lot of people.

Some of the people I considered friends started to act differently to try and fit in with everyone else. There was a point where I thought I was the problem, so I tried to fit in too.

By seventh grade I was over it!

Not only was I trying to fit in, I was also trying to fit in with a group of kids where it felt like they barely noticed me.

So, I stopped trying to fit in and started to realize who my real friends were. I found that group of friends was smaller than before. The main thing about friends trying to be different to fit in with everyone else is they ditch you... and this can cause problems unfortunately.

Some arguments with friends are stupid. I can't remember a single argument I may have had with Janiyah, Bree, or Lauren. I'm sure there have been a few though. But if I can't remember it, then it must not have been that important.

Can you remember an argument with one of your friends? If you can, it was probably serious, or really hurt your feelings. Hopefully you were able to squash the situation and remain friends. In second grade, two boys in our class liked the same girl, and these two boys were actually best friends. So, one day at recess they got into a fight. No one really knows how it happened, or what words were said to spark this fight, but there was friction in their friendship and the whole class could see it. Eventually, they made up because they were friends.

Friends do fight. It is normal, but make sure that the friendship is not one-sided. Make sure that you are not the only one putting in the work to make the friendship work.

JANIYAH

Let's not beat around the bush. All friends fight. It is a part of any friendship, fellowship, or relationship. I hate whenever I have a fight with my close friends or an acquaintance. But they happen. I had disagreements, mainly outside of my close friends' group.

When I was younger, a classmate would never leave me alone. Whenever I was trying to do my assignment, they would talk and interrupt my concentration. Then they would say I was being mean to them, when in reality it was the opposite. They would create their own story of what happened and it would lead others to believe them.

There are some teachers who will believe one person over another without getting the facts. In this situation, I am grateful the truth was revealed. I didn't feel like I had to defend myself when the adults were around. They could see the truth in the midst of everything going on. Even with having support, I still felt disappointment, anger and some-times I even cried. My parents were supportive and I learned an important lesson through this experience. I recognized that not everyone who calls you "friend" is a friend. This is one of the many reasons I value my friendship with Lauren, Sheridan and Bree.

There also was an incident where I was a bystander in a fight. A literal fight. During recess on a warm day, two boys in my class wrestled while almost everyone on the play-ground cheered them on. I did not cheer. I almost felt like laughing when I realized they weren't playing, I wanted to break them apart. But I didn't want to get hurt by two boys who were kicking, punching, hitting, pushing, and shoving.

Soon the teachers who weren't paying attention broke up the fight. Then everyone was sent to the principal's office, including me. The room became darker and stuffier the more

I stood there. Because of the 30 kids who were there and the fear I felt. However, I didn't get in trouble since I was just a bystander. I didn't do anything to receive punishment.

There was another thing that happened to me that isn't so much a disagreement or an argument. More of a squabble. In K-5, we had something called The Jacket Club. This club consisted of people who owned a school jacket. If you owned this jacket, you were considered a cooler person than anyone else.

When I asked once to play with the people who were in The Jacket Club, they turned me down. Saying, "You need a school jacket in order to play with us." Discouraged, I waited to take my case to "The Court of Thornton" so my parents, the gracious judges, could help me with The Jacket Club. The verdict came back a YES.

I got my jacket when I was in first grade, but by then The Jacket Club was over. I was still grateful, however. This experience made me realize how exclusivity could make you feel and I try my best not to do this to others. I feel my parents are my main source of information for everything, and I know I can come to them whenever I need help.

Maintaining Friendships

BREE

Maintaining friendships can be hard sometimes. You can be best friends with someone for five years, then end up losing contact because people go in different directions. When I left our old school, I wanted to maintain all of my friendships. I wanted to be able to talk to them and make new friends at the same time. It wasn't too bad at first. I still talked to most of them but, as months went by, it became harder to stay in touch. We had a class group chat which kept us talking and communicating for at least a year. The chat included a core group of my classmates who had been together since K-4.

With some of my friends we could go months without talking and then if we saw each other, we would just start talking every day again. My friend Brianna and I were really close. From Pre-K4 to third grade. We stopped talking because she moved to another school. Then in sixth grade our friend Allison invited us both to her birthday party. Brianna and I had not talked since third grade, but when we saw each other, we talked like we were best friends. Like no time had passed by. After the party was over, we would FaceTime almost every day, and are still friends till this day. We get to hang out every once in a while.

I know that we can go from friends to acquaintances quickly. Sometimes I wonder, *is this friendship going both ways? Or am I the one constantly checking up on and calling them*? If I do feel like I am the one always calling or texting them, then I just stop texting for a few days. I would test the friendship. If they didn't call, I figured out that person was not really my friend. I don't believe you should chase anyone, or that a friendship should be one-sided. It doesn't mean that we can't be friends, but I realize that they are just an associate.

If I feel that one of my friendships is drifting apart, then I reach out to them, and ask If we can FaceTime in order to see how they are doing. I do have friends I can just call, even if I haven't spoken to them for four months, and we have a great conversation.

LAUREN

Maintaining friendships. Probably one of the easiest hard things I've done. Maintaining friendships was kind of hard considering I was swamped with basketball, which kind of controlled my whole life. I had to go to practice four days a week; Girl Scouts on every fourth Friday, choir on Thursdays —all this in addition to juggling homework.

Although being at school made things easier with all the switching between the two schools. I guess you wouldn't necessarily call it 'momentous' switching, but it was switching nonetheless. School was a big part of helping me maintain my friendships. I would see my friends at school and we would chat there whenever we had time.

When leaving my old school with Sheridan, Bree, and Janiyah; the newer relationships I had developed in third grade were now strained. I didn't know the new students as well. I tried to FaceTime occasionally with one of my new friends that I made that year. We did FaceTime a few times, we actually couldn't find time for each other anymore which was really sad, but as of now we still talk occasionally.

When switching to my current school, I actually found quite a few ways to talk with my friends. They had a Bible study on Wednesdays, and I would try my hardest to make it whenever I could. We would learn about God and also have fun and catch up on all the things happening with us. This was all before the pandemic. Sometimes I'll have text conversations with them. They're really long and wordy and deep in detail. I remember all their birthdays and although, I don't have loads of pictures of them, I still give them a shout out whenever I can.

Going back to third grade, when I had made new friends with some of the new girls, there was one particular friendship that was really one-sided. (I'll talk more about it in the next chapter.) It was more like a therapist-client relationship.

She would always vent to me about whatever it was she was facing and I would always have to listen but I would never get to talk. We used to FaceTime occasionally, but then I realized she was more of an acquaintance. Which leads me to distinguish between an acquaintance and a friend.

To me, a friend is someone I can always talk to about anything, at any time, and without bothering them. Honestly, that's what I have with the rest of the girls' writing this book. So, identifying an acquaintance is just someone I occasionally talk to and don't hang out with often. To really know this difference is actually very important. Because when you know you have a strong group of people to fall back on, it really helps boost your confidence in anything that you do.

SHERIDAN

Maintaining our friendships was a little more difficult when most of the class left. When we weren't seeing each other every day, we didn't talk as much. So, we were more dependent on birthday parties and casual meet-ups. This was moreso coordinated through our parents. I didn't get my own cellphone until the summer after fourth grade, going into fifth grade. Therefore, I couldn't communicate with the rest of the class as easily up to that point.

One thing I think was a very important lesson I learned at our school was forgiveness. If someone does something to upset you, you have to be the one to get past it. If you keep letting what that person did mess with your head, then that is not good for you. You can forgive but may not forget. Just keep in mind the person's character and values if they have upset you.

Working through a disagreement is important. If you think you did something wrong, then just apologize. Otherwise, you should have a conversation with that person and try to work out your issue. You can practice forgiveness by covering the emotions you may be feeling, and then thinking about what the other person did to make you upset. Remember that forgiveness is dealing with you more than the other person and letting go of negative vibes or feelings that the person may have caused you.

I think one important thing I learned was how to treat people with respect, and to not always expect respect in return. This is to say, treat others how you want to be treated, but know that you won't always be treated the same in return.

True friendships are ones that feel like a natural connection and are not forced. True friends will stick up for you in any situation. True friends will never be jealous of your accomplishments. I'm so happy that the girls' I'm writing this book with are my friends.

JANIYAH

Maintaining friendships is something that is necessary. The way I work through disagreements is to simply talk to whoever hurt me. I have experienced friendships that are not like the ones I have with Sheridan, Bree and Lauren.

Many times they would do things that real friends

wouldn't do. In those situations I often found myself praying about it, examining my heart and talking through my feelings with my parents. Praying about it and sharing my feelings always brought me to a place of *peace*. By holding onto my peace, it made it easier when I talked to those individuals about the situation and also makes it easier to forgive. Which leads me to my next subject.

Practicing forgiveness is something we encounter almost everyday. It's really something that we have to practice the act of forgiving others makes room for us to be forgiven. It takes time and effort, but forgiveness is the only way.

Forgiveness is a decision to release resentment towards a person who has harmed you: physically, mentally, or emotionally. I have had to forgive and be forgiven. This is why forgiveness is so important. Our friendships are important and being quick to forgive makes it easier to maintain them.

True friendships are especially important. Sometimes you need someone to relate with, to hang with, and to have fun with. True friends don't do things that would hurt someone. True friends think about someone else's interests and feelings before their own. I've had my trials in trying to find out who are true friends and who are associates and acquaintances. The one thing I've observed and learned is that true friends will be there no matter what.

Changes

BREE

One weekend, my parents asked us if we wanted to leave the school. It was the summer of third grade going into fourth grade. We wrote our answers down and put them in a basket. My older brother and I wanted to leave the school, but my twin wanted to stay. I knew I would miss my friends, but I wanted a change in life. Well, I'm not sure if it was that I wanted a change or that I was just curious. I wanted to experience how it felt to be the "new kid." I also knew that some of my friends were leaving, and I did not want to get left behind at the school.

We actually agreed to stay one more year, even though there were more votes for leaving than staying. So, I tried to make my last year the best, knowing I would be making a big transition the in the fall. My fourth-grade year went by quickly and I was sad about leaving my friends.

So, it was the first day of fifth grade and I was very nervous. I had to ride the school bus for the very first time. I was glad that I could sit with my twin brother. The school was so big and there were kids everywhere. It was very different from the small private school that I went to. During those first weeks of school, I would follow my brother around because I didn't like to ask where things were. I was not an outgoing person, and I didn't like talking to people first. So, I spent the first few days not talking to anyone except my brother and my teachers.

Before I made friends at the school, I wanted to go back to my old school. Initially, I regretted choosing the option to move schools, but then I started making friends during that first week of school. I was at recess standing next to the monkey bars alone. Someone came up to me and asked my name and if I wanted to play with them. Her friends became my friends, and we had this little friend group. I started opening up and being myself around them.

I still missed people from my old school. I was pretty sure they felt sad just like me, because we were all super close. I remember once my friend cried on the last week of school because she was transferring schools and some of us were staying. So, I knew she would miss us. With transferring schools, I expected people to come up and talk to me, and that is how it went. The same thing happened at my old school in the first week too. I would not want to change anything from my experience of moving schools. I felt like we would have to leave there at some point, but we just felt after fourth grade was our time.

I already knew what it was like to have good friends. So, when I met new people, if I felt bad vibes then I would just keep myself away from them. I was doing fine at my new school and was not worried about anything until later in the year. We were walking from lunch and a teacher pulled us from the hallway. We were on lockdown for two hours. My friends and I were shaking and worried, sitting in the corner. Other people were sleeping.

Someone was moving the doorknob, and I thought to myself, *why? This would never happen at my small private school,* and *I should have never moved to a large public school.* Teachers did everything they could do to protect us and no one got hurt, so it was fine. I later found out that they were checking to make sure the doors were locked and that all of us were safe and secure. I'm glad that they protected and cared for us. It's just the world we live in. That was one of the times I thought I wanted to go back to my old school, but I just tried not to think about it too much. If I had to have that experience, at least I was there with friends who were in my class.

I am still at that school now and I love it. Some of the people I met on my first day are still there too. We are still friends, and I have made more good friends throughout my four years of being there. This is my last year, and I have to restart the process of adapting to a new school again. Especially because I am moving from middle school to high school. But I am glad that I know how to adjust to new people and new places. I can be confident that I can do it again when I get to high school.

LAUREN

It was around third grade when things started to change. Classmates left, one of our teachers had gone to pursue a cooking career, and there no longer was a high school. I had joined the soccer team. Two people left our class, but it was still a loss though since we missed them. We still carried on with our normal antics or whatever you want to call our adventures.

At the start of fourth grade, three new girls joined our class. They were all really nice. I had befriended one of them, and we had actually grown really close. As for the other two girls, I was acquainted with them, but we weren't necessarily besties. So, our class had three new kids in it, and a lot of times we would talk at the lunch table or play random games. Sometimes we would think back to our Pre-K days, and say, "Oh yeah, the *OG K-4 Squad*," and the new students kind of feel left out. The only way I would know was because they would ask to be honorary members of the squad. We said, "Sure," but in our minds we wanted it to be exclusively us.

I think I remember some bullying, as well as internal

drama, between me and another one of the new girls. She had gotten first place in the Science fair, and I got second. I think I actually befriended the person who was bullied during the last half of the year. To be honest the friendship wasn't really all that great. It was mostly one-sided. It would just be me letting the other girl vent but then not being able to talk about anything with me at all. I really didn't have anything to talk about, to be honest, but it would have been nice to just chat about anything else other than her problems.

Then suddenly my mom comes to me and is like, "Hey, you're going to go to a new school." I'm just like, "Wait no, I like it here. Why can't I be here until the eighth grade?" My mom said I needed to be challenged more, and so the process of me enrolling to a new school began. When I told my friends, they were sad because mostly everyone was leaving. There would only be two girls left from the *OG K-4 Squad.* One of them being Sheridan.

I remember making a promise to come back if I didn't like the new school. It was actually one of the constant thoughts in the back of my mind while at my new school. Then the end of the year came, along with Field Day. That year it was somewhat saddening, since there was this kind of looming thought of it being the last time we would ever hang out together. That threat was debunked though when we started having annual Christmas parties.

I moved to my new school. I was really scared because of how big the building was. I claimed that I would get lost on the way to the bathroom. I soon learned that the two people who had left from the third grade were also at the school, so I already had some friends there! I stayed for two years before I got accepted into a program that allowed me to go to independent and private schools in the DMV area.

That process was just as scary because I missed out on a lot of things in my last year at the new school. It was kind of discombobulating for me because I was really starting to fit in at that point. I sat through a whole summer of SAT training and eighth grade Math (which is admittedly more confusing now than it was before). Once again, I had to tell my friends that I would leave. They were sad, but I got all of their socials and, as of now, we still keep intact.

I had a lot of choices but eventually got it narrowed down to two: one in D.C. and one in Virginia. I really liked the one in D.C. However, it only went to eighth grade and not up to 12th grade (at that point I was in sixth grade). So, I chose my current school. I've been here now for two years and I am loving it so far. Now that I think about it, if I had gone to the other school, then I would have to enroll again into a new high school. Which I don't find ideal for me. I think that concludes everything. I'm glad I picked the school that was the right fit for me.

SHERIDAN

In our book here I guess I'm known as 'the girl who stayed at the school.' I have been there for all ten years. I've seen older students and teachers leave and new students and teachers come in. I think the most changes came in two different years. Fourth grade and seventh grade were some of the most difficult years for me.

Fourth grade was when we started learning division, which is what I struggled with for a long time. Also, that was when a lot of our classmates including Lauren and Bree left. Which meant for the next year (fifth grade) there was only me and one other girl in the class. From a social perspective, I remember I enjoyed fourth grade a lot in the middle of the year. We had a fun classroom, a fun teacher and a big class. Towards the end of the year however there were some kids talking about leaving. This was kind of sad for me because I knew I wasn't leaving. At the end of the school year there was standardized testing, and I never liked those tests.

In fifth grade I actually applied to a Performing Arts school. I went through the auditioning process and everything. I got in and was so excited, but then decided not to go because I figured it's only a few more years. Now, being in my last year, I realize how fast time goes by.

In seventh grade, three more girls joined our class. Between all the kids in our B-class, and all the kids in the A-class, there were like 20-something kids. Close to 30 in total. This just meant that there was more class drama. I didn't really care, because I was almost never involved, but it seemed like that's all kids really talked about.

Overall, I'm glad I stayed at ECS, but sometimes I wondered what I would be doing if I had made the decision to switch schools that year. But since it was a Performing Arts school and I stopped dancing the next year with my studio, it worked out. I often talk to my mom about a lot of the things happening at school. I enjoy that because she listens to me and would sometimes give some advice.

If I had the chance to do everything over again, I would wish I was a little less of a push-over. I didn't like saying no. Sometimes friends would ask me to do things for them I didn't really want to do, but I did them anyway.

I think my experiences have definitely made me who I am. I have learned so much in ten years at ECS. My experiences taught me different things that I can put in my "tool-box" for life.

JANIYAH

I've always liked being challenged with my schoolwork. Usually at private school they would give me challenging homework and schoolwork. But in second grade, when I was eight years-old, all of that changed. Everything was cool for the first couple months of school, but then I started to realize I wasn't being challenged to my fullest abilities. This caused me to worry and have curious thoughts about what I would learn or should I say not learn. I continued to analyze every possible solution. This upset me.

I was challenged every once in a while. Those moments I cherished. Meanwhile, when I wasn't being challenged, I thought to myself, "What is the point?" However, it was a requirement if I didn't want to be left behind in the second grade as a nine year-old. I told my parents how I felt and the reasons why.

My parents had already asked me if I wanted to be home-schooled. I would often cry and say, "No, I want to be with my friends." Yet now I was considering it. A family decision was made. I was going to be homeschooled.

I was upset at first because I thought I would never see my friends or teachers again. My parents reassured me that while I'm homeschooling, I would still be able to attend play-dates, birthday parties, group outings, and I could visit my old school to see my friends and teachers. I was still upset though. For almost four years I'd walked the hallways, played on the playground, joked in the cafeteria, and most of all, had special memories with people who were my second family. That was hard to just let go.

To this day, my senses hold onto the memories of ECS. The clacking of high heels down the hallway; the intercom static before the morning announcements; the bragging from students; the security guard who always said hello whenever I came through the door. The teachers telling students not to run in the hallways, and the smell of education with fellow students. The bond was strong between everyone there.

After I started homeschooling, it was a little harder than I expected. But I told myself that I could do anything. I realized that I was more satisfied with homeschooling than going to *any* school. Another thing that made me really excited about my new education was homeschool groups or co-ops. These groups are like schools for homeschoolers. They have extra-curricular activities like theater, sewing, crochet classes, cooking and more.

My expectation of homeschooling was not the reality. In reality I got to visit my friends, I was challenged like I should have been, and my homeschool groups helped me make new friends so that I wouldn't feel lonely. This is my sixth year homeschooling and I am so glad I am still doing it.

Party Time

BREE

One of the things that kept all of us together was all of the fun parties. We had so many parties I can't even remember them all. One of the places we would always go to was an indoor bounce house in our local area. Everyone would go to that location. I could not go one month without getting an invitation to a *Pump it Up* birthday party! Everyone loved having parties there when all you are doing for an hour is sliding down a slide over and over again and jumping in a bouncy house with your friends. Then going into a room to sing happy birthday and eat pizza, a slice of cake and socialize.

My first actual birthday party with them was at a swimming place. It was my fifth birthday party. At the time, I didn't even know how to swim, but we had the whole place to ourselves and it was the best pool party *ever*.

My next party was a 'girl's day'; a spa day in my basement. We all wore matching pink robes and put cucumbers on our eyes. The cucumbers felt so weird. We also put yogurt on our faces. We were confused by this and asked, "Who puts yogurt on their face?" then laughed.

Later that day we had ice cream. My mom set up a table with vanilla and chocolate ice cream, sprinkles, caramel syrup, chocolate syrup, gummy bears, and crushed Oreos. We sat down on the couch eating our custom-made ice creams and blasting the Disney channel. *Ahhh*. Disney Channel was the best with all of its funny shows. Party time was soon over, and parents started picking up their children. One of my friends started crying because she did not want to leave. She asked her mom to spend the night, and even asked me what size clothes I wore so she could wear my pajamas to sleep. But her mom told her she had to go and couldn't stay.

There was a really fun time I remember with Janiyah, Lauren and Sheridan. I had a girl's outing on a Friday in the summertime. On our way to the movie theater the four of us had to squeeze in the car. I sat in the front seat for the first time because there was no way I could fit in the back. I forget what movie we watched because I fell asleep, as usual. The chairs are too comfortable not to fall asleep in.

Later that day we went back to my house and ate pepperoni and cheese pizza from Papa John's. It was a sleepover, so we tried to stay up all night long. At the time, slime was pretty popular, and we were playing with either purple or blue slime because those were the only colors I had. I got some stuck to the blanket. I tried to hide it, but my dad found it a few days later. Anyway, the next morning we went to Starbucks and I got a S'mores Frappuccino. We sat outside at a small table and drank our yummy drinks. We had to get back so Sheridan's dad could pick her up.

A few months after that I was celebrating my birthday. I had a slime/craft party because like I said slime was very popular back then. I loved making slime so much I bought two gallons of glue. One of them was regular white glue and the other was clear. First off, we made our own shirts. Mine did not look good and you could barely read it. I made at least two or more things of slime. I used clear glue, contact lens solution, and food coloring. For the other ones I used white glue. Afterward, we hung out in the basement and only one of my friends from the party spent the night.

A few years back we tried to do a book club. I can't even remember the name of the book because we barely read it. We only had two meetings. At the first one we read a little bit, and then someone mentioned the ice cream place nearby so we just stopped reading and went there. We ended up hanging out more than reading.

The second time we met in the same place. Again, we only read a little bit and then we went to the movie theaters. The girls watched *Wonder Woman* and the boys saw *Star Wars*. The last party we had was at a gaming place for someone's birthday in September. It was like a reunion, because we hadn't seen each other in a while. Our parties helped us form a solid friendship built on fun, lots of laughs and unforgettable memories.

LAUREN

In the category of parties, we have one subcategory that was a staple to my childhood: class parties. Class parties were a completely different breed of parties. Specifically, *our* class parties. They were all overboard, ranging from your average pizza-party to penguin parties. Now that we've discussed the range, it's only fair that I rank them and everything in between.

Starting at number five, we've got your average class pizza-party. We would eat in the classroom because, if the other kids saw us eating pizza, they would be jealous and get sad. But speaking from experience, when you know that a class is having a party and you're not (and then they start bragging about how great it was), you already are jealous and sad. Not a great experience.

Moving on to number four, we have your ice-cream party. Now these parties were brief but they were always great. It would sometimes go hand in hand with the pizza-party, which only adds to the FOMO of the other classes. In my opinion, they always had the best toppings, and the gummy bears would always hit. It never fails to satisfy.

Now here's where we break into a subcategory of class parties, as these would range from penguin parties to Pi parties. Moving on to number three... the penguin party. This was not your average black-attire party. They actually happened twice in our class. We had done a project in kindergarten, where we each got a different penguin and waddled around the building.

However, the second time was much better because there was no project connected to it. We watched *Mr. Popper's Penguins* and then came up with a theme song for our class that matched the movie theme. I actually think Sheridan was the most responsible for this as she came up with it. It went *Mrs. Parker's Penguins, Mrs. Parker's Penguins...* although it was more musical and not in text form. But, since there's no audio, I'll leave it up to you to figure out what it sounded like.

Which brings me to number two... the Pi party. We had gotten our hands on (mostly) any pie you could imagine. A play on words, a play on homophones, a play on pi... (That one was good, don't deny it.) You may be wondering, "What was the reason for this party?" Well... I actually don't remember, but I do know that the mathematical number, pi, had reached some monumental value. (In numbers and not money cause that would just make you lose money, right?) But anyway, Mrs. Parker thought it was cool so we just went with it.

Now this would be at the top of the list, but what's at the top beats any party you could imagine. You could even call it a staple. At the top of my ranking in the number one spot, we have those sugar cookies with the really sugary frosting on top. Now this is controversial, only because some people don't like them, but that's unimportant. My mom going to the local Safeway, because she forgot about a party, we had the next day, was the peak of elementary school. No questions asked.

SHERIDAN

Ahhh, class parties. Our class parties were fun. We always had something to do, great food and snacks to eat. We would dress up in pink and red for Valentine's Day, green and red for Christmas, play music, go to the gym or outside to the playground… it was so much fun. I looked forward to our class parties.

My favorite kind of parties were the birthday parties. One of my favorites was Janiyah's ninth birthday party when we went go-carting. I had never been on a go-cart before and remember trying to be responsible and practice my driving. I was going slow yet fast enough, so I wasn't blocking the people behind me. I will never forget the feeling of the wind blowing in my face, the smell of gasoline and the taste of cake from her party.

Another one of my favorite parties was my first laser tag party for one of our other classmates. I remember having to wear this heavy gear while holding a heavy laser gun. When we went inside the laser tag room, it was so dark I could barely see. I had no clue what I was doing the whole time. I was so lost. I just followed the people who were on my team. I didn't hit anybody the entire time I was in there, but I had a lot of fun.

This part isn't as exciting, but presentations were a given in school. I was never super nervous in a presentation unless

I hadn't prepared for it too much. Now some kids got so nervous during presentations that they would start laughing from nervousness. The whole class would then bust out laughing. Our teacher would have to tell us to calm down, so we could get the presentations over with, I guess.

In October of 2019, the four of us decided to meet up. We met at a restaurant just to hang out and catch up. The next time we met up at a coffee shop. It was wintertime, and I remember getting a mango-mint-peach tea mixture. It was really good. You could really taste the mint and every time I took a sip of tea, I could feel the warmth filling my entire throat. We have met up every month since then. When we got together in August 2020, we decided to write our book. We were all so excited!

JANIYAH

Everyone likes to have a good time. Going to a birthday party or a group outing would make me so excited, I couldn't wait to get there. I have many memories from birthday parties that I have thrown, and that I have been to and enjoyed. Parties are a way to get to know people better. The first birthday party I remember is my own.

It was my first birthday party with friends, so I was very excited. We had a Moon Bounce party and I had a lot of fun with my family and new friends. We ate pizza, and then everyone sang "The Happy Birthday Song," which everyone knows so well, and we ate cake afterward. I still remember a lot from that day. The laughing of the kids running down the hall, the smell of ooey-gooey cheesy pizza, and the excitement of opening all of my presents. Everyone remembers those special moments.

Another birthday party I remember is Bree's birthday party. She had a New York City themed party because New York is her favorite city. We had face masks, got our nails painted, and had a dance party. Then we watched TV and played games for the rest of the party. It was so, so much fun to have a spa day with some of my best friends.

There were other ways we liked to celebrate, even without a birthday party. Lauren, Sheridan, Bree, my sister, Nevaeh, and I went to a concert with our moms. The concert was so much fun and the night flew by. After the concert, we had a meet-and-greet with the artist herself! I was really excited because she was one of my favorites.

We went into the concert when it was fairly bright outside and came out when it was completely dark. Whenever we have a good time, the hours just fly by. After the concert, we went to a fast-food restaurant named after a farm-related nursery rhyme. I had fries and ice cream. It was a wonderful way to end a wonderful evening.

Group outings are a way to spend time with the people you love. Another party I remember is my K-5 graduation celebration. This event happened to be on my fifth birthday. My class and I went on a cruise that sailed on a small river. The whole time we celebrated our graduation, everyone knew it was my birthday. Even strangers. I thought that was the best thing in the world at five years old.

We sailed the river of dirty water and my mind kept

thinking there were dolphins swimming underneath us. Afterward, we danced the afternoon away. Enjoying some delicious food, the company of each other, and the feeling of a graduation celebration and birthday party in one. The feeling of excitement and joy made the day that much sweeter.

Quarantine Life

BREE

We have been quarantined for a year now. But first off, quarantine is when you have to stay home to prevent the further spread of an illness due to COVID-19, which is a deadly virus. As I am writing this, it is March 13, 2021—exactly one year after everyone's lives changed. It was on that day my school announced they would be closing for two weeks. They had to clean the entire school to make sure the building was free of the Coronavirus also known as COVID-19.

Everyone was excited, including me, because we thought it would just be for a couple weeks. It would be a break from the building. But little did I know we were not going back for the rest of the year.

Each teacher first gave us assignments that would keep us busy for two weeks. So, two weeks passed by without being in school. I thought we were going back in April, but they kept adding weeks to our virtual school. Still, I hoped that we could go back soon. It had been a month without seeing my friends and being out of the house. Eventually we had to sign in to Zoom every day at 11:35 AM to get our work and instructions.

For each assignment, we would have to get over 70% to pass the last quarter. We would not be given an actual letter grade. The teachers would put "P" for pass and "F" for fail. The school year finally ended, and we were stuck in the house because of the COVID-19 pandemic. COVID-19 is a deadly virus and people with medical conditions have a higher chance of catching it. That is why we wear masks and we social distance which means we stay six-feet away.

I like to think about the last time I went out of the house before we were quarantined. It was around March 7th, for my friend's birthday party at Dave & Buster's. It was crowded, and we had to wait in line for tickets to play games and get a table. When I think about it, I am glad that I did not get sick at the time, because that was before we wore masks.

One of the things about being at home all day, every day, is you would need a lot of groceries, toilet paper, and just items to live. When getting water from the store, we were only allowed to take two. It could be two cases of water or two bottles of water. A lot of shelves were empty at grocery stores. Especially in the toilet paper aisle, which caused a nationwide toilet paper shortage. Anything we could find we would get. It didn't matter if it was Deer Park water or Fiji water. We wanted a certain brand of water, but we had to buy whatever was available. And my mom complained because she couldn't find enough wipes and disinfectant spray.

The first time I left the house during the pandemic was in late May. I went to a big popular store, picked up a few things and ate pizza. It wasn't much, but I was so glad to go somewhere... anywhere...

When I got tested, we were in a car and they put a very long Q-tip sized stick up my nose but not as far as the second time. I was tested a second time in August. They had to put the stick far up my nose and count from one to five for each nostril. That was the most uncomfortable and longest tenseconds of my life.

During the summer, Black Lives Matter became an even bigger thing. I went to a peaceful protest during quarantine. It felt good to yell "Justice for George Floyd" and "Black Lives Matter." This was because so many lives of innocent, people were lost. When the protests was going on, there was tear gas and rubber bullets. But when Trump supporters stormed into the U.S. Capitol, there was a different outcome. I believe Black lives matter because people of color seem to be targeted more than others.

During quarantine, one thing that happened was I actually turned thirTEEN. I went to my twin brother's baseball game and he won. I also got my hair braided in lemonade braids and my nails done. We also got a custom-made "my favorite things" marble cake. On top was pictures of me dancing, my Croc shoes, money, lasagna and TikTok.

When the quarantine started, you could not go anywhere of course. Even if you had extra-curricular activities, you could not do them. For me it was dance. We had to do Zoom calls for ballet and technique.

As of right now, I am still doing the Zoom calls for dance. They have opened the studio back up, but I am still deciding whether or not I should go back. Even though we would be socially distance. I really miss my dance friends, but I have not yet returned to the studio.

Now I am trying to learn volleyball, because I want to try a new sport. So why not try something new while I am at home?

LAUREN

When the pandemic hit, I was glad. Mainly because my Spring Break had been extended to the whole month of March, but also because I liked indoors. I remember finishing a series, ruining my sleep schedule and playing *Roblox* with my friends. When we went back to school virtually in April, everyone seemed confused and puzzled or 'confuzzled' if you will. Class wouldn't start until five minutes later because some people couldn't find a link... and sometimes the teachers even forgot to start the meeting.

There was one instance where my History teacher forgot about us having class for twenty minutes. The whole time my class and I were texting each other in our group chats, and trying to figure out what was going on. No one would turn their cameras on. It would be at least 13 out of 15 students with their cameras off, and only one or two with them on out of pity for the teacher (I was one of them).

Our first virtual family event was for my granny's birthday. I was at my cousin's house, and my mom was going over to my granny's so she could have lunch with her mom and sisters. I had to start the call at 6:00 PM because they were eating at five. Everyone came on the call, and it felt like we were all together.

Out of all my classes from seventh grade, I think my favorite was Art. Like the majority of my classes, our Art class got switched to virtual mode. I think that was my favorite class virtually because I got to make cool stuff. I made a 3-D cardboard truck, a mobile, and my favorite: the collage project, where I made a collage. Meanwhile the school year was slipping by, and the next thing I knew I was live streaming the end of the year assembly (not a sentence I thought I would say). Then summertime came and I spent a lot of time indoors.

My mom and aunt wanted to become health icons and said, "We're going to walk daily!" Since then, at least five days a week, my aunt and two cousins come over around six in the evening and we walk around my neighborhood. During the day, I would FaceTime my cousin sometimes and we would watch shows together. We watched *Avatar: The Last Airbender* and *The Legend of Korra* on Netflix. Two of many beneficial shows in my childhood.

Around this time George Floyd was also killed, and the Black Lives Matter movement started to pick up again. I had become sort of a mini activist in my family. I would make sure they would participate in Blackout Week (the week of Juneteenth) where you would not spend money at specific businesses on specific days of the week. I had also posted a lot of social justice posts on my Instagram story. I remember getting a call from my aunt after I had shared the Blackout Week with her. She told me I was going to do great things. If that's not a good enough take away from the pandemic, then I don't know what is.

SHERIDAN

We started writing this book in late 2020. I believe in September, more specifically. Before COVID-19, we would meet at restaurants just to catch up with one another. But in March 2020 the lockdown happened. We did Zoom calls for our meetups in March and April. Then decided when it got warmer outside that we could meet up in an open parking lot and practice social distancing. I enjoyed our parking lot meets because we still had the chance to see one another and still use COVID guidelines.

March 13th was a day that forever changed the world. To me, March 13th was our last "normal" day in society. For many students, that was the last full day of school. We were told we would return to school in two weeks. Two weeks then turned into a month, and then another two weeks was added... then another, and another, until we reached the end of the school year.

The remainder of the school year was held online. In all honesty, I was very aware that we were in a global pandemic where people were dying and families were losing jobs. It was definitely difficult for the whole world.

In those last three months of online school, I enjoyed doing school from home. It seemed like in previous years, that is what I always wanted. I think that the remainder of the 2019-2020 school year was not as structured, which might be why the last school year seemed easier. I remember my class schedule for seventh grade was so simple. I had Math and Science on Mondays and Fridays, English and History on Tuesdays and Thursdays, and we had Wednesday as a "development day," so we didn't have class on Wednesdays.

I can barely remember anything from summer 2020. We had been in quarantine so long, the days started to mush together. I do remember during that summer how Black Lives Matter became an important issue in America. George Floyd's death was a large contribution to the Black Lives Matter movement.

George Floyd was just one of many innocent black people to die in just that year alone. I remember seeing videos of riots on social media and in the news. I was genuinely scared that I, a young black girl, or another person of color could be the next victim of racial injustice.

For me, personally, I consider a highlight of 2020 and part of 2021 to be the election. The whole thing was a hot mess if you ask me! People were already hot from Black Lives Matter movements in prior months. There were even more protests, leading up to October and through January. Once again, I had fears about the election.

I remember thinking if President Joe Biden won, then supporters of former President Trump would go into rage and protest. But I also feared that if former President Trump won the election, the country would also protest and suffer for an additional four years.

So many questions filled my head throughout the election. But I will say this: I was loving all the memes trending on social media. My personal favorite from the vice-presidential debate was when former Vice-President Mike Pence had a fly in his hair.

The next school year came, and I was an eighth grader. I was a little disappointed at the beginning when I found out we wouldn't go back to in-person or hybrid school. I was mainly disappointed because there was a lot I was looking forward to in this grade. Since I personally had been at the school so long, I looked forward to being like the "seniors" of the school.

Around the second quarter of the school year was when I started to think I probably won't be going back to school in person. I continued to get my work done, but it was frustrating sometimes. I would get headaches from being on the computer for eight or so hours. After school, I would take a short nap to rest my eyes and clear my head. Then I'd do some homework until around seven, which is when I usually eat dinner. Afterward, if I didn't finish my work, I would then stay up usually somewhere between 10 PM and midnight to finish it.

January rolled around. I had just gotten off of Christmas break and, let's face it, was not ready to go back to school. But on January 20, 2021, a new leader would take the office. I must say having President Biden come in to clean up some things is awesome, but I think it is so important that we also have our lovely Vice-President, Mrs. Kamala Harris, in office. I know that something as simple as her presence was important for women and girls all over the world to see—our first female, and woman of color Vice-President.

I didn't have to attend school the day of the inauguration. I was glued to the TV from seven in the morning until eight in the evening, watching the entire process of the singers, poets, and fireworks at the end of the day. Earlier in the month there was the storming of the U.S. Capitol. I remember hearing about it on social media, and then talking to some friends at school about the tragic event. I couldn't help but think about what the difference would be if there were Black Lives Matter supporters storming the Capitol—how differently security would have been set up.

I remember seeing people stealing statues and taking pictures with officers. Even one lady being walked down the stairs as they rioted our nation's capital. I knew for a fact that Black Lives Matter supporters couldn't even come close to the Capitol like that. There was tear gas and violence even at peaceful Black Lives Matter protests.

I really find current events topics interesting. They strike conversation! When I get older, I actually want to study Broadcast Journalism and report the news or even write for news companies someday.

I think being in this pandemic especially for teens has taken effect on us. Some of us were told "these are the prime years of your life, have fun and enjoy them." Yet we have to be in quarantine and social distance. It just makes it more difficult for us to have the same experience generations before us had. I often hear my dad talk about how much fun he had when he was younger, especially in high school. He made friends when he was my age that he is still close with now, and who are close with our family. I hope that I can have that someday too.

JANIYAH

This past year has been a rollercoaster of emotion, uncertainty, and self-exploration. It was a change for myself, my family, my friends... everyone around me, and ironically a change for people who live on the other side of the world. Literally, the whole world changed in late March of 2020. I'm not afraid of the virus, I was just afraid of not seeing people ever again. Of course, that's not the case but hey, I thought so at the time. It was like a Sci-fi movie. Everyone having to wear masks, hazmat suits, face shields, and more.

Face masks, hand sanitizer, no toilet paper, and people buying all the frozen food. Oh my! I think that is funny. But don't worry people! We have plenty of toilet paper, and bleach, and sanitizer, and toilet cleaner, and disinfectant, and wait did I mention bleach before? My family has never cleaned this much in my entire life. Still, cleaning has not been the only thing that has affected me.

This quarantine has affected me emotionally as well. I miss getting to go to my Homeschool groups where I performed theatre, where I expanded my mind a little more, and just hung out and talked with close friends. I don't even know when I will be able to go back to my Homeschool group. I miss being able to just coordinate excursions with a number of friends, and without having to follow government guidelines in order to see other human beings.

I was in my feelings a couple of times. I almost couldn't take the fact that I had not seen my friends and most of my family for six months. I'm so glad that I am able to see some of my family and friends now. I even get to see Lauren, Bree, and Sheridan in person once a month. In a nearby empty parking lot during the summer. I missed meeting up with my friends in person. We started meeting over video calls when winter started. Hopefully we will get to hangout more because it is warmer. Now I can look forward to outings with friends, but in March no outings were allowed. It was stay home, stay home, and you guessed it—*stay home.*

No one knows what is next to come. Don't even get me started on schooling. I mean this year wasn't that much different from it usually is. I have been homeschooling for the past six years so this wasn't new to me, but my friends and their parents who selected a public or private school for education were not used to any type of homeschooling.

There has been an upside to this. I have been able to hang out with my family more. We are not as busy as we were before; everything kind of slowed down. From wrestling matches with my dad and my siblings, to movie nights, or game days—this quarantine period has given us opportunities to learn more about each other.

But this is not the only thing that happened in 2020. There were so many protests regarding Black Lives Matter, the Presidential election, and the U.S. Capitol riot. Many historical moments took place for America. I believe that many of the things they were protesting were important issues, but some of the protests did not have to be as drastic.

I do believe that I have learned something from all of this. I am more capable of doing things that I thought at first were hard. My dance technique has improved. My knowledge in school has increased. My writing skills have shown through. I am capable of anything and everything.

Our Friendship Now

BREE

Janiyah, Lauren, Sheridan and I are still good friends and our monthly meet ups kept us close. In November of 2019, we met at a bakery just to catch up and talk about how we were doing. We started meeting monthly at different places, such as a bakery or cafe, and once at Sheridan's house. During our meetings we could ask questions and talk about topics that interest us. We had open discussions about self confidence, our goals and anything that came to mind. The moms were there to offer advice and share their own teen girl experiences. We met up at least four times before the pandemic hit, and that did not stop us from being able to talk to each other.

We started doing Zooms, which is just a virtual video communication app. During the summer the four of us went to a parking lot, but we sat on the trunk of our cars. Making sure to stay socially distant. At one of these meetings, we decided to do a project together, which became us writing this book. Our monthly meetups have impacted our friendship because we didn't lose our connection. We get to know how each of us is doing. Now we are going to be co-authors AND friends.

Something unique about the four of our friendships is that we don't really argue. *About anything.* If there are any disagreements it would not be a big deal. We could forgive and forget. It takes time to earn and build trust. Both friends have to be honest. You have to show your feelings and admit your mistakes. We do not see each other or talk every day, but we are unbreakable. Not anyone or anything could ever stop us from being friends. I mean look at us... we are writing a whole book together.

The true meaning of a friendship is someone that has your back no matter what. Someone who's like family. Someone you can trust. Someone who wishes the best for you. Friendships are a combination of love, loyalty, respect, and trust. But you know what types of friends are really *friends* and right for you.

First you have to gain trust by really understanding who the person is. I am really grateful to say that I can trust Sheridan, Janiyah, and Lauren. They have shown me what real friends are since the day we all met.

There is a difference between a friend and an associate. A real friend will be right there for you whether you are at your happiest or your lowest. They will check up on you no matter what; they will love you behind your back and in your face.

An associate is someone that you don't have to talk too often. They are not really checking up on you, and you are not checking up on them.

LAUREN

When I heard that we were meeting up, I was excited. I had a feeling that it would feel like any other time we hung out outside of school. But since we weren't all at the same school it would only be slightly different. I think our first meeting was at a cafe. I remember the location being really packed and us waiting 15 minutes for our food. We hadn't really come up with any topics, so we were just catching up and talking about anything.

I think we also had our journals for us to write letters to God. I remember soon after we got the journals we went to the window and waved at passersby in their cars. We would cheer when someone would wave and boo when someone wouldn't. There was also a police officer patrolling the parking lot and, whenever we would see him passing by, we would turn around and act like we weren't doing anything.

I also remember another meeting at Sheridan's house about self-identity. We met Sheridan's pet bird in person for the first time. After that, we were just talking in Sheridan's room for at least 20 minutes. I have noticed there's a cycle with all of our meetings. We catch up with all the other mother-daughter duos, and then talk about a subject for at least 30 minutes. Then we would separate from our mothers and talk about random stuff.

Then the pandemic hit and we were forced to go virtual for our meetings. It saved us a 40-minute drive, but it was kind of sad as well. We had to get used to using Zoom for our meetings. There were multiple occasions where we would just talk for hours. Those meetings would end because there was some sort of trial for Zoom. Where every time you started a Zoom call, it would only let you have an hour-long meeting.

After a couple months of that cycle, I put out a "semi-illegal" (my own phrasing from June 2020) idea. We would socially distance and sit in our cars and hold the meetings in person. Our meeting cycle would continue as before we would break into our little cliques after 30 minutes to an hour of discussing things. I remember one time we were bored so we raced to the end of the parking lot. Janiyah says otherwise, but I definitely won that race. Bree placed third, while Sheridan pulled in last because she didn't have the right shoes.

Eventually we had to go back to the virtual meetings because the weather had gotten colder. By that point we had decided to write this book. Luckily, the weather is warming up and soon we'll be able to get back to seeing each other in person.

SHERIDAN

I remember when we first started our meetups. It was November 2019, and we first met at a bakery. We first just started catching up and talking about school and sports, and our personal lives. But my favorite part of that night was when we would look out the window of the bakery and wave at the cars passing by. We would laugh when someone waved back at us.

I was happy to reconnect with some of my oldest friends. I feel that all of us being at different schools, has affected our friendship. We weren't seeing each other every day and communication between the four of us, and the rest of the class that left wasn't as consistent at the time. I just enjoyed coming back together. We laughed, shared old jokes, and reviewed old memories.

I'm sure my mom could tell you how much I was rambling in the car before the meet-up. I was excited. I remember making sure my outfit was just right for the occasion. At this one meet-up we decided to come together once a month somewhere. The restaurant meet-ups were short-lived due to COVID. I definitely think that us meeting once a month made it easier for us to stay in touch. After we started our monthly meet-ups, the four of us would text or call during the week.

I feel as if our friendship is special. We have all shared at least one hobby in common at one point in our lives, so we could always talk about it. We all danced. Some of us did competitive dance and some danced at school or with other programs.

Since we were at the same school at a young age, we could laugh and talk about all of our memories from previous years. We have been friends for so long, there is definitely trust between us. I feel like I can tell my friends just about anything. Whenever we talk, our conversation comes naturally. It doesn't feel forced or awkward, which I think is awesome.

With a lot of our friends leaving the school over the years, and me personally being one of the few who are left, I had to realize that not everyone is your friend but an associate. An associate is someone with whom you are cordial, but you don't exactly feel like sharing every detail in your life. A friend is someone you know you can always count on. You can tell them just about everything, and they will do the same. A true friendship is when you are honest with each other, no matter how difficult.

JANIYAH

When my friends and I reconnected, I was so excited. Our friendship remained the same. It was almost as if we had talked yesterday and just continued our conversation. We have always been like that. Even during quarantine, we talked more than ever before. I think that is great. We reconnected in November of 2019. We got together in a bakery and decided just to catch up and talk about what was going on in our lives.

My mom contacted the other moms to coordinate a meetup for all of us girls. We still meet monthly now, on Saturdays. That day is the emptiest day in all of our schedules. Our friendship is different just because of the length of our friendship. We will have known each other for ten years in September. We have a different bond compared to my other friends. We can even finish each other's sentences. We don't talk behind each other's back.

I personally had an experience where someone was gossiping about me, and the things they were saying weren't even true. I can talk to Lauren, Sheridan, and Bree about anything. I also have their trust to tell them what is on my mind. I think that trust is an important factor in friendships. We have built our trust by not doing things that we wouldn't want someone doing to us. We understand and value our friendship. We wouldn't want to do anything to hurt it. I believe a true friendship is recognizing others' differences, and not discounting things that are comparable and the same. Having each other's backs. Being willing to forgive and willing to ask for forgiveness.

What's Next?

BREE

When the pandemic is over and we don't have to worry about COVID-19, I want to be able to go to my high school every day. I really want to have face to face interactions with everyone when I start high school. I learned how to adapt to change from fourth to fifth grade. But my concern is having to make friends through a Zoom screen if we are not able to fully go back to the classroom. I hope I don't have to meet people virtually because my only option is to email them and this would be awkward. I'd really want to get to know someone in person.

I know there will be loads of work—even though I wish it wasn't. So, if I don't procrastinate and stay on top of my work, I will be fine. If I have any free time during my day, I will use it wisely to complete my assignments. Because I know if I get behind on my work in high school it will be even harder to catch up.

I'm not sure what to expect when I return to my class for the last few weeks of middle school. Most of my friends will continue virtual school. I wanted to do virtual for the rest of the year, but my parents want me to finish middle school with hybrid learning.

It's time to get ready for all the new people I will meet next year. I know not to let negative people faze me. I still don't understand why people like being so rude.

Like, what is being mean doing for you?

I learned how to choose my friends wisely by making sure I can depend on them, and they can do the same for me. Making sure they have good character and that they can be a good influence is important.

I never would've seen myself writing a book, and I'm not even in high school yet. But I am happy that I stayed motivated to finish this book, while doing school projects, essays and many assignments. Not many people our age would want to write a book or have even thought about it. But I am excited about what I've learned about the writing process and I can't wait to hold the book in my hand. This is only the beginning of what my bright future holds. We'll just have to see what comes next. Who knows? I might just write about it.

LAUREN

This chapter is relatively short considering that it's a reflection. This journey is coming to an end. As for the future, I'm kind of excited. The other day I heard an ad on Spotify saying that the end of the virus is near, but it's up to us how fast it ends. Steps we could take were keeping socially distant and getting the vaccine. I know not to believe everything I hear on the internet, but this one sounded pretty convincing. Since I can't get the vaccine, it's just like, "Oh, ok, so I have to be patient and keep doing what I'm doing (socially distancing)."

Next year I start high-school and I am sort of excited, but also worried. If we start next year virtually, we are going to have a lot of new kids in our class. This year I knew there were three new kids at school, but I didn't really know who they were until we started going in person. So, if we keep up distance learning, I feel it will be harder to socialize.

Really, with high-school, I just want to meet new people and figure out what I want to do for college. Some goals I have for myself are just upgrading my relationship with God and becoming more independent. By 'independent' I mean keeping track of my time and being more responsible. I've also learned how to stop procrastinating. I guess my silver lining is that I'm being proud of the person I'm becoming. Although I have no clue what I'll be doing in the future, I know God's got me. That's good enough for me.

SHERIDAN

I am, overall, really happy that we decided to write this book. I hope that this can be inspiring to someone else. I'm glad for the chance to write it with my friends.

Next year I start high school. I am nervous, but mostly

excited about what is to come. I have struggled with meeting new people during this quarantine. The last time I made a new friend was at the beginning of the seventh grade.

My parents always said to be careful making friends online, because it isn't reliable. I just hope that when I enter high school, the pandemic is more under control. Then I can go back to in-person learning, which will make it easier to meet people my age.

I think it is really important for kids our age to learn that not everyone will like you. There are going to be kids who have nothing better to do than to pick on you. When I get into high-school, I won't really care about people who are rude and unpleasant. People try to hate just to bring you down or to see your breaking point.

Don't try to fit in with people who won't help you grow as a person. It might be something you regret later. It's always good to try and make friends, just make sure you choose your friends wisely.

If school is still online next year, I'm not sure how I will make new friends. I didn't have to make new friends at school this year because there were no new kids in our class. I already knew everyone! Mrs. La Tashia (Janiyah's mom) often mentions a toolbox. Basically, a toolbox is the information and skills you have to prepare you for certain situations. I know in my toolbox, I have judgement skills. I have the ability to read someone based on how they talk to others, how they walk, etc.

One of the most important things I have learned during quarantine is that in the end, you always have someone or something to depend on. Even if you think you don't. If you feel like you have only yourself to depend on, remember there is someone who is going through something similar to your situation. I am grateful to have learned this lesson and have my friends and family to depend on.

JANIYAH

This year was interesting, and the situation was not what I expected. I mean it was great because I learned many things about myself but, at the same time, I wanted the coronavirus virus to be over. Many memes came out this year because of this event that changed the entire world. But honestly, you guys can make memes about something else.

Like, seriously. I think everyone in the world had to be more creative. I mean, you've got to find things to do when you're stuck in the house. When it takes two weeks to mail something eight miles away from your house. When everyone else in the world has to do the same thing you're doing: Staying at home!

During the pandemic I started an online Homeschool group. I literally met people from England and Uganda. It's kind of crazy. I even met someone who once lived in the same area as me. Traveled the same roads I did. Went to the same Homeschool group that I went to. That is so crazy. So, I am grateful that I got that experience. I just wish that the coronavirus would stop causing all this chaos. What a way to end my middle-school years.

I am literally going into high school in September 2021. I

hope that the Lord will help me choose my friends, know my enemies and the ever-popular frenemies. I think if I do meet new people through virtual learning, there will be a way for me to contact them outside of class like I already do. I mean, nowadays there is text, phone calls, video chats, offline chat, emails, and the oldest form of communication... *letters.*

Oooh, ahhh!

I believe that even with all of this technology, social events can still be possible. As long as you follow government guidelines, wear a mask, wash your hands, and that's right... you guessed it—*stay at home.* I will need some sort of a social event so that I am not just focused with SCHOOLWORK. The assignments, papers, science lab reports, presentations, quizzes, tests and lesson plans. *I mean it.* So much so that I could accurately stack up my books and assignments and it would reach my bedroom ceiling.

Although the schoolwork is a bit extreme at times, this is the best schedule I have ever had. My schoolwork is done accurately and regularly. My grades have become invariable. I am very satisfied with my progress in eighth grade. This is my last year in middle-school. I had to learn how to manage my time and I had technology to help me. Online documents, drives, and journals. I even have a regular old planner with a calendar. But, if I am being completely honest, I don't use my planner. Although I should use it more often.

It is almost unbelievable that I will be in high school in September. I am a little nervous, but also excited. When I was little and I walked the halls of ECS, I dreamed of the day that I would start high school. The day I would be taller than other kindergarteners and look upon them to give them words of wisdom and carry on the next generation.

Even though it's hard to believe that I am going to high school, it not hard to believe that I have goals. My goals are to take all Honors classes. It may sound hard but I believe in myself and I accept the challenge.

School is not the only goal I wish to accomplish. I plan to start a YouTube channel and start my own business. When I become a performer, I will share my gifts and talents in a way that will glorify my Heavenly Father.

With the knowledge I have learned from my parents, grandparents, teachers, and friends, a hope of mine is to spread joy throughout a world filled with negativity. With the help of my Heavenly Father, I will have the courage to reach into my toolbox and select the tools I need to make my life prosperous, plentiful and joyous.

Made in the USA
Coppell, TX
27 July 2021